Christmas

PROGRAM BUILDER NO. 52
Resources for the Creative Program Director

Recitations • Monologues • Sketches

COMPILED BY PAUL M. MILLER

Unless otherwise indicated Scripture quotations are from the *Holy Bible, New International Version*® (NIV®). Copyright © 1972, 1978, 1984 by International Bible Society. Used by permission of Zondervan Publishing House. All rights reserved.

Permission to make noncommercial photocopies of Program Builders is granted to the purchaser when three books have been purchased. The photocopies cannot be sold, loaned, or given away.

Copyright © 1999 by Lillenas Publishing Co. All rights reserved.

Cover design: Paul Franitza

Lillenas PUBLISHING COMPANY
KANSAS CITY, MO 64141

Contents

Recitations 4
    Preschool 4
    Ages 6 to 8 7
    Ages 9 to 11 9

Plays, Monologues, and Programs 11
    The Shepherd's Story, by Kipp D. Wilson 13
    Joy to All: An Alternative Advent Wreath Ceremony,
        by Esther M. Bailey 17
    Parties and Plays, Dreams and Visions: A Christmas
        Play for Young Teens, by Andria Phillips 20
    All You Need Is a Willing Heart:
        A Play for Cast and Choir, by Sandy Mercer 30

Recitations
PRESCHOOL

Welcome!
I'm not very tall,
I'm not very wide.
But here's my big welcome,
To all here inside.
—*PMM*

Welcome
Friends and neighbors, moms and dads,
Sis and brothers too;
Glad you're at our program,
We'll do our best for you.
—*PMM*

Welcome
Glad you're here
With Christmas cheer.
—*PMM*

Last Call
We welcome you one,
We welcome you all.
Come and sit down.
It's the last call.

We may be little,
We may be small,
But we have been asked,
To welcome you all.
—*Amy Spence*

Extra! Extra!
(Child carries a newspaper in one hand and a newspaper bag around his or her shoulders filled with rolled up newspapers.)
Extra! Extra!
Read all about it!
There's a [Christmas] program tonight,
So how about it?
Stay for the singing;
Stay for the show;
Stay for my lines;
Please don't go!
Extra! Extra!
Read all about it!
There's a [Christmas] program tonight,
So how about it?
—*Amy Spence*

Very Happy
I'm very happy
Christ is born;
Rejoice! Rejoice!
It's Christmas morn!
—*Robert Colbert*

Now You Know
Christ is born,
Our Savior and King.
Now you know
What Christmas means!
—*Robert Colbert*

True Meaning

CHILD 1: Be happy! Be thankful!
  Christ is born.
CHILD 2: And that's the true
  meaning
BOTH: Of Christmas morn!
  —Robert Colbert

Good News!

(Child enters with newspaper held high.)
  Good news! Good news!
  It's Christmas morn.
  Tell everyone
  That Christ is born.
  —Robert Colbert

My Gift

  My gift to the King,
  I will gladly bring.
  I'll let everyone see,
  My gift is me!
  —Wanda Brunstetter

The Tiny Angel

The tiny angel on the tree
Reminds me of God's love for me.
The angels sang and told the news,
About the babe—King of the Jews.
  —Wanda Brunstetter

Snowflakes

(Four small children enter, each carrying a large glittery snowflake.)
CHILD 1: Lightly the snowflakes fall,
  whirling all around
CHILD 2: Soon we will see a blanket
  of white on the ground.
CHILD 3: Jesus' love is like
  snowflakes so white,
CHILD 4: It can cover our sin, right
  here, tonight.
  —Enelle Eder

In Each Heart

  In each heart
  On Christmas morn,
  May Christ our Lord,
  And King be born.
  —Robert Colbert

Jesus Joy

(Little girl enters as Mary. She carries a doll.)
  Christ was Mary's baby boy,
  Born to bring us Jesus joy.
  —Robert Colbert

A Cradle

  In a little manger
  Lay a tiny stranger.
  —Mary Ann Green

We Can

  We can tell of Jesus' birth.
  And how He came to us on earth.
  —Mary Ann Green

Happy Birthday

  Happy birthday, dear Jesus,
  Happy birthday to You.
  We love You, dear Jesus,
  And You love us too.
  —PMM

Tall

I may be smaller than some.
I may be taller than some.
But I sure will not holler like some.
(Whispers) Merry Christmas!
  —Mary Ann Green

Abiding Love

  He came from heaven above
  To give us each abiding love.
  —Mary Ann Green

I'm Not Big

I'm not very big,
But, I've a huge wish for you.
May your Christmas be merry,
And may mine be too.

—PMM

Come to Him

(Five small children enter, each carrying a picture.)
CHILD 1 *(with picture of an angel):*
  Angels came in robes of white,
  Singing praises on that night.
CHILD 2 *(with picture of shepherds):*
  Shepherds came to share the joy,
  Of finding Jesus, the baby boy.
CHILD 3 *(with picture of barn animals):*
  Animals came on quiet feet,
  To see the little child so sweet.
CHILD 4 *(with picture of the wise men):*
  Wise men came from lands afar,
  Safely guided by the star.
CHILD 5 *(with picture of church):*
  We, too, can come to worship Him,
  Just as they did in Bethlehem.

—Enelle Eder

Recitations
AGES 6 TO 8

Christmas Cookies

(Four children enter. One carries a cookie sheet with cookies of the shapes called for: Christmas tree, star, bell, boy/girl. As CHILD *speaks, he or she picks up corresponding cookie.)*
CHILD 1 *(takes cookie off sheet):* Ever eat a tree?
    All covered with glitter and ice?
I think I'll eat one now,
(Takes a bite)
    Hmmmm, that's nice!
CHILD 2 *(takes cookie off sheet):* Ever eat a star?
    I've picked one from the sky.
I think I'll eat it now,
(Looks at cookie)
    Hmmmm, good-bye!
(Pops whole cookie into mouth)
CHILD 3 *(takes cookie off sheet):* Ever eat a bell?
    A tinkling Christmas bell?
I think I'll eat one now,
(Pops whole cookie into mouth)
    Ohhh, well!
(Takes another one and eats it)
CHILD 4 *(taking cookie off sheet):*
    Jesus loves the little children
    All the children of the earth,
He sent His Son, the Christ child,
That we might have new birth.
(Puts cookie into pocket and pats it gently)
                    —PMM

Sing a Song of Christmas

CHILD 1: Sing a song of Christmas,
    Let your joy be heard;
Telling of the Savior,
    According to God's Word.
CHILD 2: Sing a song of Christmas,
    Just like the angels sing;
Glory in the highest,
    To the newborn King.
CHILD 3: Sing a song of Christmas,
    Throughout the silent night,
Of the blessed Savior
    Who came to bring us light.
CHILD 4: Sing a song of Christmas,
    A song of peace and joy,
And the story to be told,
    Of a precious baby boy.
CHILD 5: Sing a song of Christmas,
    Setting your thoughts apart;
To bring honor to the One,
    Who can dwell within your heart.
(Children may sing Christmas hymn.)
                    —Enelle Eder

No Manger for Me

I like to go to Grandpa's barn
And play around in the hay;
But when it gets dark and cold
    inside,
I do not want to stay.

Though Jesus slept where the
    animals fed,
I do not want to sleep in a stall.
A donkey nibbling on my pile of hay
Might leave me no bed at all.

Yet I know that God cared for His
    Son,
And kept Him from Herod's
    sword,
So if I ever have to sleep in a barn,
I'll pray and trust the Lord.
—*Margaret Primrose*

Where Is Baby Jesus Now?

(Sing to the tune, "London Bridge Is Falling Down.")
Where is baby Jesus now?
Jesus now, Jesus now?
Where is baby Jesus now?
Up in heaven.

He is there for you and me,
You and me, you and me.
He is there for you and me.
Up in heaven.

Jesus wants us all to come,
All to come, all to come.
Jesus wants us all to come.
Up to heaven.

Ask Him into your heart today,
Heart today, heart today,
Ask him into your heart today.
So you can go to heaven.
—*Amy Spence*

Recitations
Ages 9 to 11

The Shepherds

I wonder how the shepherds felt,
   On that cold and lonely night;
When the silent curtain of darkness
   Was broken by heavenly light.

Did they want to run away
   When the gleaming angel
     appeared?
Did their hearts beat loudly
   Despite the warning not to fear?

And when they made the journey
   To little Bethlehem town,
Did they know what waited inside
     the barn,
   That Messiah would be found?

What joy they must have felt
   To be chosen for a part.
What memories they must have
     kept
   And treasured in their hearts.
         —Enelle Eder

Christmas Comes A'Calling

With a crispness in the air,
   And laughter in the street;
Christmas comes a'calling
   To everyone it meets.

Folks are telling secrets,
   Their hearts all full of joy.
Total excitement is mounting
   In every girl and boy.

This is a season of love,
   Of peace and of goodwill;
When our Savior came to earth,
   His Father's promise to fulfill.

Among the fun and gaiety,
   Let us pause to recall
The real reason for the season,
   When Christmas comes to call.
         —Enelle Eder

Conversation About Giving
A Dialogue

(Boy and girl with long wish lists for Christmas. They speak to themselves and check the items off.)

JONI: Let's see, now, I have my Barbie list, my clothes list . . .

TONY: And I have my Nintendo list, my action figures list, my video list, my . . .

JONI: Now, here's my sports equipment list. Let's see, it includes new in-line skates and a blue gymnastics outfit, and . . .

TONY: Whew, close call—I almost forgot to add a micro-close-up lens for my camera. *(Writes)* "Available from Acme camera shop on Broadway."

JONI: I thought I put Press-On nails and a '50s skirt with a fuzzy poodle and chain . . . oh, here they are. While I'm at it, I should tell Dad about the pre-Christmas sale at Johnson's Hobby Shop. They've got Barbie 4-wheel drive Jeepsters on sale . . .

TONY *(looking through the lists):* Did I remember to put a lighted yo-yo on my stocking list? *(Looks up and sees* JONI*)* Oh, hi, Joni. Whatcha doing?

JONI: Oh, I'm making out my Christmas gift list. You?

TONY: I'm doing the same thing. What're you giving your little sister?

JONI: Who?

TONY: Your little sister? You know, that little blond girl named Sara who lives at your house?

JONI: Oh sure, Sara. I don't know what I'm giving her.

TONY: I don't know what I'm giving mine, either. Boy, it's tough to pick out just the right gift for someone else.

JONI: Right you are, but that's what Christmas is all about, isn't it?

(Blackout)

Plays, Monologues, and Programs

The Characters of Christmas
Monologues by Wanda E. Brunstetter

Mary's Story

I'm Mary, the blessed one.
   God sent an angel to me
With a message of hope
   That would set the world free.
The angel told me great things;
   That I would deliver a son.
He would be God's child,
   The chosen One.
I was to call Him Jesus,
   Son of the highest;
A reigning King—
   I felt so blest.
Later, I went to Bethlehem
   With Joseph, my betrothed.
We traveled with others,
   To pay the taxes we owed.
There was no room in the inn,
   Is what we were told;
We went to a stable,
   So dark and so cold.
But God kept us safe,
   And I delivered a son,
We named Him Jesus,
   So that prophecy was done.

Joseph's Story

I am Joseph of Nazareth,
   A man who trusts God.
An angel appeared to me,
   And I thought it was odd.
He told me that Mary,
   The girl I planned to wed,
Was carrying a baby boy—
   "Conceived by the Holy Spirit,"
   he said.
"Call his name Jesus,"
   The angel told me,
"He will save the world,
   From all sin that will ever be."
So I woke from my sleep,
   Then took Mary as my wife.
I knew she'd make me happy
   For the rest of my life.
Mary and I went to Bethlehem
   To pay Caesar our tax;
There was no place to call our own,
   And so I couldn't relax.
Then we were taken to a stable,
   Where animals were fed and
   slept;
I think that in her tiredness,
   Mary could have wept.
Amid the stock, in that humble
   place,
   My wife, she birthed a son;
He was the Savior of the world,
   Who came for everyone.

The Innkeeper's Story

Remember me? I ran an inn in Bethlehem.
That fateful night my rooms were full,
So I sent a pregnant lady into the night
    To sleep with lambs of wool.
I later heard she'd given birth
    To a son inside a cave
That wasn't fit for humans—
    Oh, she was so very brave.
The word around our neighborhood
    Was whispered she'd born God's Son.
I heard that there were shepherds
    Who entered the dismal stable, one by one.
They'd left their sheep and everything,
    To come and see their brand new king.
And rumor had it that some angels
    Even came to sing.
I wish I'd made some adjustments;
    Maybe moved some people out,
To accommodate that special birth—
    He is our King, I have no doubt!

The Shepherd's Story

by Kipp D. Wilson

Cast:
>SHEPHERD: *older man; one of those who saw the newborn Messiah*
>MAN: *a skeptic*
>WOMAN: *taunting and sarcastic*
>MARY: *sympathetic*

Costumes: Rough peasant clothes; more European feel than biblical

Setting: An inn in Bethlehem four months after Jesus' death. A table stands center stage with three chairs.

(At rise SHEPHERD *sits at the table in the center seat. He holds a mug and drinks introspectively.* MAN *walks in, looks around, and sees an empty chair beside* SHEPHERD.*)*

MAN: Excuse me, Sir. May I sit here?

SHEPHERD: Yes, please sit and join me.

MAN *(sitting):* Thank you. *(Looks around impatiently for a waiter. Finally yells.)* Innkeeper! *(Frustrated)* I hate coming to a puny town like Bethlehem. The service here . . .

SHEPHERD: Excuse me, Sir. Are you from Jerusalem?

MAN: Jerusalem? No. I'm sorry, I'm not. Why do you ask?

SHEPHERD: I was hoping for someone to tell me news of the Messiah's coming.

MAN: Messiah? What are you talking about?

SHEPHERD: The prophets tell us that when He appears, Messiah will enter Jerusalem riding on a donkey. I keep waiting for news of that happening.

MAN: And you think He's going to appear soon?

SHEPHERD *(excited):* I have seen Him already! I was there when He was born.

MAN *(incredulously):* What?

SHEPHERD *(reminiscing):* It was just as the angel told us. It was such a humble place—a stable outside of town in the middle of nowhere. And there He was, so small, so innocent; just a little baby. But even then, you could sense the presence of God in Him. It was as though God himself shed His robes of purest light and took on the body of an infant.

MAN: Sir, look—I don't know who you are or what you saw . . .

SHEPHERD *(not hearing):* I asked His mother what His name would be. She told me that an angel of the Lord appeared to her and told her the child's name. Because He would finally prove to all the world that our Lord is the God who saves, she should call His name Jesus.

(MAN *reacts negatively.*)

MAN: Wait a minute! Are you talking about Mary and Joseph from Nazareth? The carpenter and his wife?

SHEPHERD: Why yes, he said he was a carpenter in Galilee. *(Excited)* Why? Do you know them?

MAN: Oh, I know them, all right. And their Son, Jesus. Some Messiah He was.

SHEPHERD: What do you mean?

MAN: I grew up in that rotten little town. I knew Mary and Joseph; I even went to synagogue with Jesus. He seemed pretty normal then. Then He left Nazareth, and that Messiah thing started.

SHEPHERD: But He is the Messiah! You don't know what I saw . . .

MAN: You don't know what I saw, either! You see, He came back to Nazareth to preach in the synagogue. He started giving us all this talk about how He was the Son of God—the anointed one. Well, excuse me, but I remember He was the Son of Joseph the carpenter.

SHEPHERD: But . . .

MAN: And you know all those stories about the miracles He did? Nothing. I didn't see Him work a single miracle there. Everyone in town got so angry at Him, we finally threw Him out. So don't tell me He's the Messiah.

(WOMAN *enters looking for a place to sit.*)

SHEPHERD *(upset):* You don't know what I saw! I know He is the Chosen One! And when Jesus does enter Jerusalem . . .

WOMAN *(interrupting):* Jesus? You mean Jesus the Galilean? The one who claimed to be the Messiah?

SHEPHERD: Yes! Do you know Him?

WOMAN *(sitting):* I just came from Jerusalem. They're still talking about Him.

SHEPHERD: Then He has come!

WOMAN: Oh, He came, all right.

SHEPHERD: Then the time of the Kingdom is at hand!

WOMAN *(smirking):* You haven't had any news from Jerusalem, have you?

SHEPHERD: No, I haven't.

WOMAN: Maybe you'd better get the whole story before you go announcing that the kingdom of God is here.

SHEPHERD: What do you mean? You said the Messiah came to Jerusalem.

WOMAN: The Messiah? Let me tell you a few things about your "Messiah." This person comes riding into town with His 12 henchmen, not a single scribe or rabbi among them. He goes into the Temple and starts vandalizing it. Then, He turns around and curses all the religious leaders of the city!

SHEPHERD *(doubting himself):* But the angel that appeared to us that night told us He brought good tidings and great joy. He said that this baby was the Christ.

WOMAN: Did he also tell you that your Christ was going to be killed by the Romans?

SHEPHERD *(aghast):* What?

(MARY *unobtrusively enters and stands to one side listening to the conversation.)*

WOMAN *(with relish):* That's right, old man. The Pharisees called Him a heretic and the Romans called Him a traitor. So they hung Him up on a tree, nailed His feet and hands there, and watched Him die. Then they threw His body in an empty cave and rolled a stone over the opening. *(Sarcastically)* Hallelujah.

SHEPHERD *(trying to convince himself):* But you don't know what I saw . . .

(WOMAN *gets up to leave.)*

MAN: Get it through your head, old man. A false prophet who couldn't work miracles, and a criminal who couldn't save himself—that's your Messiah.

(MAN *and* WOMAN *leave.)*

SHEPHERD: The angel. The angel was wrong. It was all just a lie.

(MARY *crosses to* MAN *and sits beside him. The* SHEPHERD *doesn't notice her.)*

MARY: Excuse me, Sir . . .

SHEPHERD *(wrapped in his thoughts):* It must have all been a dream.

MARY: Please, Sir, I overheard what you were saying just now . . .

SHEPHERD: How could I have been so wrong?

MARY: Sir, please, I have to know. Did you see the birth of the Messiah?

(SHEPHERD *is shaken out of his reverie. In fear of more persecution, he answers.)*

SHEPHERD: No! I didn't see anything.

MARY: Please, it's important. You were in Bethlehem the night He was born, weren't you?

SHEPHERD: I don't know what you're talking about.

MARY: Yes, you do. You witnessed the birth of Promised One.

SHEPHERD *(still fearful):* You don't understand. It was all a mistake. It was all a dream.

MARY: Sir, listen to me. Don't believe what others have said. They don't know the whole story. I don't know what you saw in the stable that night . . .

SHEPHERD *(jumps up):* That's right, you don't know! Who are you anyway? You have no idea what I saw that night. You have no idea who He is!

(SHEPHERD *starts to storm away;* MARY *stands.)*

MARY: Wait, Sir! (SHEPHERD *stops and turns to look at* MARY.) My name is Mary Magdalene—and I do know. *(She walks over to* SHEPHERD, *puts a hand on his arm.)* Now, let me tell you what I saw.

(Walk off together or BLACKOUT)

Joy to All
An Alternative Advent Wreath Ceremony

by Esther M. Bailey

Traditional Advent wreath lighting ceremonies take the congregation from the Isaiah scriptures anticipating Messiah, through His birth. This feature takes a more topical approach.

First Sunday of Advent

Scripture Lesson: Luke 2:10-11

Leader's Homily: There are different ways to consider the all-inclusive aspect of the good tidings of great joy. Our first thoughts often focus on the truth that God's Gift is meant for people of every nation. Indeed, this is true, but it might also be well to consider what the Christmas story means to the kind of people we meet every day—the kind of people we are: the young, the old, the ordinary, the extraordinary.

Jesus, our Friend and Savior, came into the world as a little child. Children identify with the Baby in the manger. They know that Christmas is special for them. Their faces take on the glow from the Christmas tree as they try to solve some of the beautifully wrapped mysteries that lay at the foot of the tree.

Children miss the point of Christmas, though, unless they accept Jesus as Savior. Jesus didn't come to bring presents and goodies but to live in your heart. If you ask Him in while you are a child, He will guide your entire life and keep you from the problems that sin brings on.

Children are an important part of [name of church]. This Christmas will be richer for our entire congregation because children are being introduced to Jesus.

Advent Candlelighting: As a teacher from the children's Sunday School department, I light this candle on behalf of the children of our church. As we watch the candle burn, I'd like each child to say in his or her heart, "Jesus, come to me." Wouldn't Christmas be a wonderful time to decide to ask Jesus to live in your heart always?

Second Sunday of Advent

Scripture Lesson: Luke 2:10-11

Leader's Homily: Last Sunday we focused on Christmas for children. This Sunday we're going to the other end of the age spectrum and look at Christmas from the senior citizen's point of view.

Today's Scripture lesson comes from the story of Simeon, an old man whose primary purpose in life was to actually see Jesus. So, when the parents brought the baby Jesus to the Temple, Simeon took the child in his arms and gave praise to God, declaring that his life was now complete, because he had seen the salvation of the Lord.

As adults, we recognize that our interests change with age. The joys of childhood are no longer ours to enjoy. The joys of youth are passing by.

However, as the joys of childhood and youth fade, the prospect of heaven looms brightly. It is ours to remember that life in the eternal city is possible only because Jesus came. We can make that life a reality only through accepting Him as Savior.

The scene is a nursing home. A paralyzed stroke victim with tears streaming down her face is listening to an instrumental group playing "The Old Rugged Cross." Even with the tears, the woman nods her head in agreement with the song. This is exactly what the coming of Jesus does for senior citizens. When all else may be failing, the joy that Jesus brought to the world is still theirs.

Advent Candlelighting (*a senior adult or a minister who works with them may share a meaningful experience before lighting candles one and two*): First I light last week's candle for children. It still burns brightly. Now I light this second candle on behalf of the elderly who attend [name of church], and those affiliated with our church who are unable to attend. Let's bow our heads and have a moment of silent prayer for our active senior adults and for our shut-ins. May all senior citizens witness the salvation of the Lord in a personal way before this Christmas season is over.

Third Sunday of Advent

Scripture Lesson: Luke 2:10-11

Leader's Homily: We have already learned that these good tidings are extended to people of every age. Today, we consider the promise from the standpoint of social structure. Most of us are rather ordinary people who'd like to be assured that the message is for us too. Fortunately, the original recipients of the angels' message provide that assurance.

If the lowly shepherds in a field outside of Bethlehem deserved a visit from angels, then there is no doubt that that same message extends to us. The coming of Jesus into an individual life is just as spectacular today as was the announcement of His birth to the shepherds. These rustic people, like folks today, were plagued with troubles, but personal problems took second place when they came under the influence of God's glory and the plan of salvation.

The wonderful part of the invitation to ordinary people is that after we accept God's gift of love, life isn't ordinary any more. When the power of sin is broken, individuals are free to reach their full potential through the power of Jesus Christ. This is possible because Jesus came.

Advent Candlelighting: Again, the first candle is lit on behalf of children; the second, for our elderly; and now the third candle is lit on behalf of ordinary people like us. Join me in praying that those who do not know Jesus as Savior will allow the light of Christ to change their lives.

Fourth Sunday of Advent

Scripture Lesson: Luke 2:10-11 *(unison reading with the congregation)*

Leader's Homily: While we may identify with the shepherds' reaction to the angels' message, it is important to note that they were not the only ones included in the "tidings of great joy." We learn that from the story of the wise men. Theologians tell us that the visit signifies that salvation was to extend beyond the Jews. It also indicates that persons of wealth and influence are welcome in the kingdom of God.

Wise men and women still seek Jesus; some still dedicate their lives to His service. It is fortunate that they do because their power and influence can make life better for all humanity.

Advent Candlelighting: Since our first Sunday of Advent, this candle has represented children, the second, our elderly, the third, ordinary people. Now, I light this fourth candle on behalf of people of influence and leaders of the world, our nation, our state and city, and of our church and its staff; [names]. May the light of Christ illuminate their lives so that they may share the message of Christ with the rest of the world.

Parties and Plays, Dreams and Visions
A Christmas Play for Young Teens

by Andria Phillips

Cast: In order of appearance
    JOE: *a teen*
    MARNIE: *a teen*
    BRANDON: *a teen*
    APRIL: *a teen*
    JORDAN: *a teen*
    SANDY: *a teen*
    MRS. PETERS: *elderly neighbor*
    DUKE: *tough teen*
    SLIMER: *tough teen*
    CRUSHER: *tough teen*
    THE COBRAS: *five or six teen gang members (nonspeaking)*
    JESUS: *our Savior*

Playing time: Approximately 25 minutes

Act I
Scene 1

Setting: High school hallway and cafeteria

Time: A week before Christmas

(JOE *enters UL [up left],* MARNIE *from DL [down left]. They wear coats and are carrying schoolbooks. They meet and continue across stage to cafeteria DR [down right].)*

JOE: Hi, Marnie!

MARNIE: Oh, hi, Joe!

JOE: Ready for Mr. Baxter's algebra test?

MARNIE: I hope so. I know the material. I'm just kinda bummed out this morning.

JOE: Yeah, I know what you mean. Being at church half the night working on the Christmas program really tired me out too.

MARNIE: Mrs. Turner is such a perfectionist! She must have had me say *(raises arms angel-fashion),* "Behold, I bring you glad tidings" at least 150 times!

JOE: And I'm sure I have a permanent callus on my knee from dropping to it at the manger so many times. I can see it all now; my son says, "Say, Dad, did you get that bum knee playing football?" And I answer, "No,

Son, I got it playing *shepherd!" (Both laugh.)* Want to stop for some hot chocolate, Marnie? There's plenty of time before class starts.

MARNIE: Sounds good to me. *(She sits at table.* JOE *brings two mugs from the counter and sits.)* I really didn't sleep very well last night. Guess I was all wound up from play practice. *(Pause, then remembers)* You know, I had the weirdest dream.

JOE: No kidding! I had one too.

MARNIE: Tell me about yours.

JOE: You're probably not going to believe this, but I was in the church in my shepherd costume, and I was kneeling at the manger. When I looked up, nobody else was there—except *Jesus!*

MARNIE: You mean baby Jesus?

JOE: No, I mean *Jesus* Jesus! *(Gestures indicating an adult size)* He was standing there by the manger, see, and He says, "Joe, I'm going to come visit you tomorrow." (MARNIE *chokes on her hot chocolate.)* Hey, you OK?

MARNIE *(still coughing):* No . . . yeah . . . well, maybe. Joe! That was my exact same dream.

JOE: You dreamed that Jesus is coming to visit *me* today?

MARNIE: No, I dreamed that He said He was coming to visit *me* today!

JOE: Righteous! Two people with the same dream!

MARNIE: Weird, huh? *(Pause)* Joe, you don't suppose . . .

JOE: I don't know, Marn. I mean, people in the Bible used to dream dreams and see visions and stuff like that. But this is the 21st century. And you and I are just, you know, kids!

MARNIE: Yeah, it's probably nothing. *(Pause)* 'Course, Mary wasn't exactly ancient when Gabriel talked to her.

(They sit in silent thought for a few seconds.)

JOE: Marn?

MARNIE: Yeah, Joe?

JOE *(jumping up):* I'm not taking any chances!

MARNIE *(rising):* Neither am I!

JOE: What are you going to do?

MARNIE *(thinking):* Well, it's Christmas—Jesus' birthday. *(Brightening with an idea)* I'm going to put together the greatest birthday party this town has ever seen. How about you?

JOE: Well, the last time anyone important visited us at school, they opened all the lockers. Mine was a total trash heap!

MARNIE: Oh yes, that was the time the school board was looking for some kind of contraband . . .

JOE: And Mrs. Heidelman, the board chairman, opened my locker, got one whiff of my gym socks, and fainted dead away! I was so embarrassed.

MARNIE: So? What's that have to do with . . . hmmm . . . the possible visit, eh? What are you going to do, you know, in case He . . . *(points heavenward)* does come?

JOE: I'm gonna go clean out my locker.

MARNIE: Right! Good luck. *(Exits SR)*

JOE: See you later! *(Exits SL)*

Scene 2

Time: Moments later

Setting: School hallway

(JOE *is cleaning out his locker, surrounded by trash cans, crumpled paper, books, clothing, forgotten lunches, etc.)*

JOE *(looking around in disbelief):* How could one guy collect so much junk in just three and a half short months? *(Looking heavenward)* Lord, I don't know if You do locker checks on visits or not, but if You do, this is one area where I sure could use an extra helping of Your mercy!

BRANDON *(enters hurriedly, SR):* Joe! Thank goodness I found you! *(Noticing the mess)* Whoa! Pig-sty City! What's happenin', dude?

JOE: Well . . . never mind. You'd think I was crazy.

BRANDON: Cleaning out this nuclear waste area without a parent or teacher standing over you with a baseball bat? I *know* you're crazy! But, hey, forget this, will you? We're having an algebra test in 15 minutes, and I need your help!

JOE: But, Brandon, this is important. *Real* important!

BRANDON: Joe, if I flunk this test, I flunk the whole semester. If I flunk the semester, my mom'll have a cow, and my dad will have a coronary!

JOE *(sigh):* OK. Show me the part you don't understand.

(BRANDON *hands him the book.)*

JOE: Brandon, this is the whole book.

BRANDON: That's the part I don't understand.

(JOE *looks toward heaven, quickly crams his things back into his locker, and slams the door.)*

JOE: Come on, Einstein. Let's find a place where we can work.

BRANDON *(elated):* Yes!

Scene 3

Time: Noon

Setting: School cafeteria

(MARNIE *and* APRIL *enter SR, carrying lunch trays.*)

MARNIE: Here's a place, April. Let's sit down. I need your help on, like, an *emergency* project!

APRIL: Look, Marnie. I'm not in a very creative mood today, OK?

MARNIE: Oh, come on. You're going to *love* this! I'm throwing *the* party of the season . . . possibly of the *decade* . . . possibly of the *millennium!* And it happens *tonight!*

APRIL: Tonight?! But . . .

MARNIE: And I want you to help me make out the guest list. We have to include just the right people, the best of the best! *(Hands* APRIL *a pad and pencil)* We'll want the student council president . . . and all the class officers . . . the cheerleaders . . . and *of course* the football and basketball teams! And . . . April! You're supposed to be writing all this down! Get with it, will you? We don't have much time!

APRIL: Marnie, I need to . . .

MARNIE: To go shopping for a new dress? Maybe we can squeeze that in right after school.

APRIL: Marnie . . .

MARNIE: I want us to look our very best. There's a special guest coming, maybe!

APRIL: Marnie . . .

MARNIE: You wouldn't believe me if I told you who, so . . .

APRIL: My parents are getting a divorce!

(Silence)

MARNIE: What?! Oh, April, what a bummer!

APRIL: You're my best friend, Marnie. I really need to talk to you about this.

MARNIE *(sympathetically):* Yeah . . . sure . . . *(Brightening back into original enthusiasm)* First thing tomorrow morning. Right now we have a *very important* social event to plan!

APRIL: Marnie! I need to talk now!

MARNIE: Now? But, April, this is *important!*

APRIL: More important than my life?

MARNIE: Well, you see . . . No, of course not. We'll work on this later. *(Puts pad and pencil away and stands)* Let's take a walk. Talk to me. Tell me everything.

(Girls exit SR, MARNIE's *arm around* APRIL's *shoulders)*

Scene 4

Time: End of school day

Setting: School hallway, by lockers

(JOE *and* MARNIE *are taking books, etc., from their lockers, preparing to leave for home.*)

JOE: Uh . . . Any sign of *Him* yet?

MARNIE: No. How 'bout you?

JOE: Not a glimpse. But I guess I'm just as glad He's waited until after school. *(Looks into locker in disgust)* I didn't get very far with my locker-cleaning.

MARNIE: Speaking of cleaning. I'd better get home. I called my mom at noon to tell her about the party, and she freaked out! She said she'd cook, but I'd have to dust, run the vacuum, clean the bathroom—and the tree isn't even up yet! I'd be so embarrassed if Jesus came to His own birthday/Christmas party and the tree wasn't even up!

(They close lockers and begin walking down the "hall.")

JOE: Is the party before or after the Christmas program at church?

MARNIE *(stops suddenly):* The program! I almost forgot! *(Gasps)* What if He comes to the program!

JOE: Oh no! I hadn't thought of that! We'd better get going. I've got to learn my lines for the last act!

(Resume walking)

MARNIE: Let's see! I have to clean, decorate, wrap some gifts, press my costume, rehearse my song . . .

(JORDAN *and* SANDY *enter SR; meet* JOE *and* MARNIE *center stage.*)

JORDAN: Joe! Marnie! Just the people we need!

JOE: Hi, guys. What's happenin'?

SANDY: The school office just got a call from the Rescue Mission downtown. You know all the food and clothing the Student Council's been collecting for them for Christmas? Well, they need it *right now!*

MARNIE: Now? We're supposed to deliver that next Wednesday.

JORDAN: It seems that three new homeless families have arrived.

SANDY: Three *large* and *hungry* homeless families!

JORDAN: And they don't have enough provisions on hand to feed them.

MARNIE: So?

SANDY: So *we* have boxes and boxes of food. And we need to get it down there, *pronto!*

JOE: But Marn and I have . . .

MARNIE *(cutting him off):* We just can't, that's all.

JORDAN: But you're the only kids around right now with cars.

MARNIE: Well, I'm sorry, but I've got to get home. Something really big may be happening tonight, and I have a zillion things to do to get ready.

JOE *(resigned):* Come on. We can use my car. I guess we can't have *real* people starving while I *pretend* to be a shepherd. Where are those boxes?

JORDAN: Great! Thanks!

SANDY: Come on. They're down by the gym.

(JOE, JORDAN, *and* SANDY *begin to exit, SR.)*

MARNIE: Oh, wait up. I can't get ready for a party while carrying three tons of guilt on my head.

SANDY: All right!

JOE *(jovially):* Come on, martyr!

(All exit.)

Act II

Scene 1

Time: 5 P.M. that same evening
Setting: MARNIE's living room
(MARNIE *is busy decorating and cleaning. Doorbell rings. Frustated by the interruption,* MARNIE *goes to answer it.*)
MARNIE *(opening door):* Oh, hi, Mrs. Peters.
MRS. PETERS: Hello, Marnie, dear. Is your mother or father at home?
MARNIE *(working as she talks):* No, Ma'am. My dad isn't home from work yet, and my mom's at the bakery, picking up some things for my big party tonight.
MRS. PETERS *(sitting down):* Oh dear. I was hoping they could run an errand for me. You see, my husband's medicine is all gone and if he misses a dose, he could become very ill. I was hoping your mom or dad might go get the prescription refilled for me. Herbert and I don't drive any more, you know.
MARNIE: Well, we're awfully busy with the party and the church program tonight, but maybe my dad can take care of it when he gets home after 6:30.
MRS. PETERS: But the drugstore closes at 6:00. *(Walks over to* MARNIE*)* Marnie, do you think *you* could go for me? I hate to ask, what with your party and all, but Herbert will be so sick without it.
MARNIE: Oh, Mrs. Peters, I'm sorry. I just can't go right now. Why don't you try the Browns across the street. They don't do much at Christmastime. Maybe they'd be able to help you.
MRS. PETERS *(disappointed):* All right, dear. *(Starts toward door)*
MARNIE: I *am* sorry. It's just that, well, there's a really important person coming tonight and . . .
MRS. PETERS: I understand . . . I hope your party goes well.
MARNIE *(without enthusiasm):* Yeah. Thanks.
MRS. PETERS *(starting out the door):* Merry Christmas, dear.
(MARNIE *watches her leaving, suddenly picks up her coat and car keys.*)
MARNIE: Hold up, Mrs. Peters. Which drugstore is it?
MRS. PETERS: Oh, Marnie, you're a lifesaver!

Scene 2

Time: Later that night
Setting: Street leading to the church

(JOE *enters SL, walking toward the church, dressed in his shepherd costume and carrying a staff. Three street "toughs" enter SR and begin to harass him.*)

DUKE (*moving upstage of* JOE): Whoa! Check it out!

SLIMER (*positioning himself in* JOE's *path SR*): It's a little old lady with a real tall cane.

CRUSHER (*passing in front of* JOE *to SL, looking him over*): No, dude. This is a shepherd. Ain't you never seen a shepherd before?

DUKE (*punching* JOE's *shoulder*): Hey, shepherd, where's your sheep?

JOE: Well, actually, they're over at 5th Avenue Community Church. (*Laughs nervously*) They're cardboard.

SLIMER (*turning* JOE *toward himself roughly*): Cardboard! Whoa! Must be a real challenge to keep them all rounded up!

CRUSHER (*wheeling* JOE *around to face him*): Sounds pretty wimpy to me. Maybe I was wrong. Maybe this ain't a shepherd. Maybe this is Little Bo-Peep!

(*Laughter*)

SLIMER: Yeah! Check out those knobby knees! (*Kicks* JOE *lightly in leg. Laughter.*)

JOE (*turns SR to leave*): Look, guys, I'm in a real important Christmas play and I'm already late, so how 'bout just moving over and let me be on my way, huh?

(DUKE *and* SLIMER *block* JOE's *way.*)

DUKE: Sheep-man wants to go find his little lambs. What do you say to that, Crusher?

CRUSHER: I say forget it, sheep-man! (*Pushes* JOE *down*) There ain't gonna be no little play for *you* tonight! (*Starts toward* JOE, *as if to beat him*)

(DUKE *and* SLIMER *look SL and begin running away SR.*)

SLIMER: Hey, Crusher, look out! Here come the Cobras!

(*Rival gang members run in from SL. Two chase* DUKE *and* SLIMER. *Others beat* CRUSHER, *then exit quickly, SL.*)

JOE (*looks around, then crawls to* CRUSHER): Lie still. You're hurt pretty bad. Here (*takes off costume headpiece to use as bandage*). Let's see if I can stop the bleeding.

(MARNIE *enters SL, wearing angel costume.*)

MARNIE: Joe? Joe, what in the world . . . ?

JOE: Marnie! Thank heaven! There's been a fight!

MARNIE (*gesturing toward* CRUSHER): Did you do *that?*

JOE: Hey, what kind of a Christmas shepherd do you take me for?

MARNIE: Is that Crusher Malloy?

JOE: I'm afraid so.

MARNIE: He looks pretty bad.

JOE: Yeah.

MARNIE *(looks at* CRUSHER *a minute longer, then turns to* JOE*)*: Well, come on. We're gonna be late for the play.

JOE: Marnie! The guy's hurt! We can't just walk off and leave him!

MARNIE: Oh, I guess not . . . although that's exactly what he'd do.

JOE: Look, you run over to that gas station and call for help. I'll stay here with Crusher.

MARNIE: OK. *(Starts to leave, but turns and backs out, talking to* JOE *as she exits SR)* But it's already 7:15. If we're late for the play and You-Know-Who comes . . .

JOE: Just hurry, will you?

(MARNIE *turns and exits quickly.)*

Scene 3

Time: 12:00 midnight

Setting: MARNIE's living room

(JOE *and* MARNIE *enter SR, still in shepherd/angel costumes—somewhat rumpled—and collapse on couch. Clock chimes 12:00.)*

MARNIE: Well, so much for parties and plays and dreams and visions.

JOE: Yeah. I guess we were pretty dumb to think God would pay a personal visit to a couple of crazy teens. It just seemed so *real.*

MARNIE: I know. But I guess it's a good thing it *was* all just a dream.

JOE: *Two* dreams.

MARNIE: *Two* dreams. Without the head shepherd and the herald angel, the program was probably a disaster.

JOE: And the police kept us so long, answering questions about the fight, that we didn't even make it back in time for your party.

MARNIE: That's OK. Most of the kids couldn't come anyway, on such short notice. *Some* big birthday bash Jesus would have had if He *had* come. The tree still isn't even up!

JOE: And I never did get my locker cleaned out, *or* my lines really learned.

MARNIE: Well, at least Crusher's going to be OK. And I checked on April before I left for the play. I think she feels a little better now that she was able to talk it all out.

JOE: *And* the three families at the mission are now large, but *not* hungry. *(Pause)* And Brandon passed his algebra test—by one point!

MARNIE: What a day! *(Silence)* Joe, you don't think we were so busy that . . . you know . . . we *missed* Him, do you?

JOE: Oh, I don't know. I'm too tired to think. Surely it was all just a dream.

(Both lean back on the couch and close their eyes. Lights dim. After a pause, JESUS *enters, softly spotlighted, and stands looking at them as they doze.)*

JESUS: No, Joe and Marnie, you didn't miss Me. You just didn't recognize Me! I was the friend who needed help with math; the one who needed comfort; the families in need of food. I was Mr. and Mrs. Peters. I was even Crusher, lying in the street. You gave Me food and comfort, healing and help. Far more precious to me than plays, parties, and decorations are these gifts of love from a servant heart. "I tell you the truth, whatever you did for one of the least of these brothers of mine, you did for me."

The End

All You Need Is a Willing Heart

by Sandy Mercer

Cast:
LITTLE ONE	MARY	BARN ANIMALS
GABBY	JOSEPH	SHEPHERDS
SARAH	FIRST INNKEEPER	ANGELS
MOSES	SECOND INNKEEPER	FIRST WISE MAN
DAVID	THIRD INNKEEPER	SECOND WISE MAN
NARRATOR 1	NARRATOR 2	THIRD WISE MAN
NARRATOR 3	NARRATOR 4	NARRATOR 5

Props:
Autoharp
Stool
Angel costumes for Gabby and Little One
Costume for Sarah
Rocking chair
Costume for Moses
Shepherd costumes
Walking stick
Costume for David
Manger
Baby
Animal costumes
Angel costumes
Wise men costumes

Setting: Word is out around heaven that God is going to send Jesus to earth in human form. LITTLE ONE, a small and inexperienced angel, thinks the idea is great but is convinced that with a little fine-tuning, God's plan could be spectacular. She talks with GABBY [Gabriel] about her ideas, but the unimpressed older angel suggests LITTLE ONE talk to some other folks in heaven who know God's ways better than LITTLE ONE does.

LITTLE ONE speaks with SARAH, MOSES, and DAVID. They can understand her feelings because of their own experiences. But each emphasizes that God's way is always best and all God wants from each person is a willing heart.

A disappointed but wiser LITTLE ONE returns to find GABBY excited because God has chosen LITTLE ONE to tell the shepherds about Jesus' birth. The now reluctant little angel is reminded by SARAH, MOSES, and DAVID that all she needs is a willing heart. As the Nativity scene is enacted, LITTLE ONE brings the "good tidings of great joy."

As the events of the special evening unfold, LITTLE ONE gets caught up in the excitement. Forgetting the lesson she has learned, she plans special appearances all over earth to tell the good news. An exasperated GABBY reminds LITTLE ONE: God's way is always best.

Scene I
The Big News

(GABBY *enters and sits center stage on a stool. He [or she] is tuning his [her] Autoharp.* LITTLE ONE *bursts onto the stage.*)

LITTLE ONE: Did you hear the big news?

GABBY: Yes, I did. Isn't it wonderful?

LITTLE ONE *(incredulously):* Wonderful? Well, yes, of course it's wonderful . . . I . . . uh . . . mean the idea is wonderful. God going to earth in human form to walk among the people to show them what He is like. Yeah, that's wonderful. But the rest of the plan stinks!

GABBY *(in a scolding voice):* Little One!

LITTLE ONE *(somewhat sheepishly):* Angels have opinions, too, you know.

GABBY: That may be, but God knows best. You must trust Him.

LITTLE ONE *(with building enthusiasm):* Oh, I trust Him. I was just thinking maybe I could offer Him a few suggestions to improve His plan. For example, the talk around heaven is that Baby Jesus will be born to a young peasant girl named Mary. The earthly father is supposed to be some carpenter named Joseph. Jesus is to be born when they go to Bethlehem for the census. Now get this! Bethlehem is going to be so crowded, with everyone coming for the census, that they won't even be able to find room in an inn. Some kind-hearted innkeeper is going to let them use his stable for the night. Do you believe it? Jesus will be born in a barn! And His first bed will be a manger. (GABBY *keeps at his [her] work.* LITTLE ONE *gets right in his [her] face.)* Did you hear me? Mary is going to let Jesus sleep on the hay that cows eat!

GABBY *(annoyed):* I heard you. But I'm afraid I don't understand the point.

LITTLE ONE *(frustrated):* OK. Listen to this. God is going to send *us* to tell some *shepherds (with obvious disgust),* you know, the guys who watch those stinky sheep, that they can find *God's Son* in a barn with some cows, sheep, and goats. Then it's going to take some wise men *(with sarcasm)* over a year to follow the star in the East to find Jesus.

GABBY *(looking up):* So?

LITTLE ONE *(flabbergasted):* So? So?! Even I could think of a better plan than that!

GABBY *(with mock disbelief):* Really?

LITTLE ONE: Of course, just listen to this. There are lots of royal families available. Pick one, King Herod, for instance. Let Jesus be born in a palace. He would have the finest bed, the softest baby clothes, and all the latest toys. On the night of His birth God could do some fancy fireworks with the stars and planets—not just one star that only wise men would be looking for. When He has everyone's attention, He could send down the angelic choir. And . . . this would be a great touch . . . He could send the Heavenly Philharmonic Orchestra! Whadaya think?

GABBY: I think you should talk to a few people who know God better than you.

LITTLE ONE: For instance?

GABBY: Well, Sarah, Moses, and David for starters.

LITTLE ONE: OK, I'll talk to them. But you'll see. They'll think my plan is better.

(LITTLE ONE *leaves the platform.* GABBY *strokes the harp one more time.*)

GABBY: We'll see.

Scene II
I'm Old and Tired and Babies Cry All Night

(SARAH *is rocking in a rocking chair on the stage.* LITTLE ONE *enters.*)

LITTLE ONE: Excuse me, Sarah. (SARAH *nods.*) Gabby suggested I speak with you about my ideas for the night of Jesus' birth. I was thinking that God . . .

SARAH *(interrupts):* No need to go on, Little One. *(Laughs)* Everyone in heaven has heard about your *new* and *improved* ideas.

LITTLE ONE *(with obvious pride):* So whadaya think?

SARAH: Perhaps I should tell you a story. A long time ago, God said to my husband, Abraham *(stands and makes a sweeping motion heavenward),* "Look up at the heavens and count the stars—if indeed you can count them. . . . So shall your offspring be" [Genesis 15:5]. We believed and trusted God. We waited many years, but we didn't have even *one* baby. So we grew tired of trusting that God's plan was best. We came up with our own plan, which ended up causing a lot of trouble for us and others. Then, when I was 90 years old, God spoke to Abraham again and said, "I will bless her and will surely give you a son by her. I will bless her so that she will be the mother of nations; kings of peoples will come from her" [17:16].

LITTLE ONE: So what happened?

SARAH: I said, "I'm old and tired and babies cry all night."

SARAH and CHOIR: I'm old and tired and babies cry all night. I'm old and tired and babies cry all night.*

SARAH: And do you know what God said to me? *(Pause)* "All you need is a willing heart."

SARAH *(repeats two times):* I'm old and tired and babies cry all night.*

32

CHOIR *(repeats four times as* SARAH *is saying "I'm old . . .")*: All you need is a willing heart.*

SARAH: And finally I answered, "I have a willing heart. I have a willing heart." That, Little One, is my story.

LITTLE ONE *(without conviction)*: Right, sure, well, thanks for talking to me.

(LITTLE ONE *exits followed by* SARAH.)

Scene III
I Stutter, I Stammer, and Pharaoh Is So Strong

(MOSES *is pacing back and forth on the stage with a big walking stick.*)

LITTLE ONE *(less sure of herself than when she met* SARAH): Moses?

MOSES *(stops and looks at* LITTLE ONE): Ah, Little One. I heard you might be dropping by.

LITTLE ONE: Word sure travels fast around here. I guess you also heard about my idea. No one seems to understand. I'm not saying that God's plan is bad—I just think if He fine tuned the plan it could be spectacular! I thought maybe you might understand.

MOSES: Let me tell you a story, Little One.

LITTLE ONE *(under her breath)*: Not again.

MOSES: What was that?

LITTLE ONE: Oh, nothing. Go ahead.

MOSES: My people, the Hebrew people, were slaves to the Egyptians. I wanted to set them free. One day, I saw an Egyptian beating a Hebrew. I could stand the unfairness no longer, so I killed the Egyptian. The Pharaoh heard about it, and he wanted to kill *me*. I was scared and ran away. I lived for many years as a shepherd *(chiding* LITTLE ONE)—you know, the one who watches those stinky sheep. Then one day God told me He was sending me to tell the Pharaoh to let the Hebrew people go. Now, if He had asked me to lead an army, well, I could have done that. But to *tell* Pharaoh to let the people go? That was out of the question. You see, I was never good at talking.

LITTLE ONE: So what happened?

MOSES: I said to God, "I stutter, I stammer, and Pharaoh is so strong."

MOSES and CHOIR: I stutter, I stammer, and Pharaoh is so strong. I stutter, I stammer, and Pharaoh is so strong.*

MOSES: And do you know what God said to me? *(Pause)* "All you need is a willing heart."

MOSES *(repeats two times)*: I stutter, I stammer, and Pharaoh is so strong.*

CHOIR *(repeats four times as* MOSES *is saying, "I stutter . . .")*: All you need is a willing heart.*

MOSES: And finally I answered, "I have a willing heart. I have a willing heart."

LITTLE ONE *(without enthusiasm):* That's a great story. Thanks.

MOSES *(reaches out to touch* LITTLE ONE): I understand how you feel, Little One, really I do.

(LITTLE ONE *exits followed by* MOSES.)

Scene IV
I'm Young, I'm Small, and Israel Has a King

(DAVID *is sitting on a stool.)*

DAVID: Hi, Little One. I've been expecting you.

LITTLE ONE *(dejectedly and with a little sarcasm):* I suppose you've heard about my *great* idea. And, let me guess. I'll bet you even have a story to tell me.

DAVID *(lighthearted, but with compassion):* I do, Little One. I do. Have a seat. This won't take long. *(After* LITTLE ONE *is settled,* DAVID *begins.)* When I was a young boy, God said to Samuel, "I am sending you to Jesse of Bethlehem. I have chosen one of his sons to be king." When he arrived at my father's house, he saw my oldest brother, Eliab. Samuel thought, "Surely the LORD's anointed stands here before the LORD." But God said to Samuel, "Do not consider his appearance or his height, for I have rejected him. The LORD does not look at the things man looks at. Man looks at the outward appearance, but the LORD looks at the heart." My father had my seven brothers walk in front of Samuel, but Samuel said to him, "The LORD has not chosen these." So he asked my father, "Are these all the sons you have?" My father answered, "There is still the youngest, . . . but he is tending the sheep." Samuel said, "Send for him." When I arrived, God said to Samuel, "Rise and anoint him; he is the one" [1 Samuel 16:1, 6, 7, 10, 11, 12]. But I was scared and I said, "I'm young, I'm small, and Israel has a king."*

DAVID and CHOIR: I'm young, I'm small, and Israel has a king. I'm young, I'm small, and Israel has a king.*

DAVID: But God said to me, "All you need is a willing heart."

DAVID: I'm young, I'm small, and Israel has a king. I'm young, I'm small, and Israel has a king.*

CHOIR *(repeats four times as* DAVID *is saying "I'm young . . ."):* All you need is a willing heart.*

DAVID: And finally I said, "I have a willing heart."

LITTLE ONE *(getting up sadly):* Thanks for the story. I guess sometimes we just don't understand God's plan, but His way is always the best way, huh?

DAVID: You're catching on, Little One. You're catching on.

(LITTLE ONE *and* DAVID *exit.*)

Scene V
I'm Little, I'm Scared, and You Have More Experience

(GABBY *is pacing back and forth on the platform.* LITTLE ONE *walks in sadly.*)

GABBY *(with excitement):* I thought you'd never get back. Just wait 'til you hear the good news.

LITTLE ONE *(with little interest):* What good news?

GABBY *(with even more excitement):* God has chosen you!

LITTLE ONE *(with increasing interest):* Chosen me? What are you talking about?

GABBY: God has chosen you to tell the shepherds about Jesus' birth.

LITTLE ONE: No way! I'm little, I'm scared, and *you* have more experience.*

LITTLE ONE: I'm little, I'm scared, and *you* have more experience. I'm little, I'm scared, and *you* have more experience.*

(SARAH *enters and stands stage right.*)

SARAH: I'm old and tired and babies cry all night.* *(Repeat four times while* LITTLE ONE *says, "I'm little, I'm scared, and you have more experience.")*

(MOSES *enters and stands beside* SARAH.)

MOSES: I stutter, I stammer, and Pharaoh is so strong.* *(Repeats three times while* SARAH *and* LITTLE ONE *say their lines.)*

(DAVID *enters and stands beside* MOSES.)

DAVID: I'm young, I'm small, and Israel has a king.* *(Repeats two times while* SARAH, MOSES, *and* LITTLE ONE *say their lines.)*

CHOIR *(repeats eight times starting piano and building to forte while* LITTLE ONE, SARAH, MOSES, *and* DAVID *say their lines rhythmically):* All you need is a willing heart.*

SARAH, MOSES, and DAVID *(speaking in unison):* I have a willing heart.

LITTLE ONE *(humbly):* I have a willing heart.

(Lights out)

Scene VI
The Nativity

NARRATOR 1: "And it came to pass in those days, that there went out a decree from Caesar Augustus, that all the world should be taxed. (And this taxing was first made when Cyrenius was governor of Syria.) And all went to be taxed, every one into his own city. And Joseph also went up from Galilee, out of the city of Nazareth, into Judaea, unto the city of David, which is called Bethlehem; (because he was of the house and lineage of David:) to be taxed with Mary his espoused wife, being great with child" [Luke 2:1-5, KJV].

(JOSEPH *and* MARY *enter as the* CHOIR *sings appropriate selection. The preschool choir enters dressed as barn animals and moves to the part of the platform designated as the stable. The three* INNKEEPERS *enter as the preschool choir sings appropriate song.* MARY *stands on the ground, and* JOSEPH *approaches the platform and speaks quietly to an* INNKEEPER. *He points to* MARY *and attempts to explain their plight. The* INNKEEPER *folds his arms and with his arms signals no.* JOSEPH *returns to* MARY. *They walk a few more steps.* JOSEPH *returns to the platform and repeats the same actions to another* INNKEEPER. *This is repeated a third time. The third* INNKEEPER *looks at* MARY *with empathy and points to the stable area on the platform.* JOSEPH *assists* MARY *and they go to the stable area.*)

NARRATOR 2 (MARY *and* JOSEPH *go to the stable area and face the audience;* MARY *picks up the baby lying in the manger*): "And so it was, that, while they were there, the days were accomplished that she should be delivered. And she brought forth her firstborn son, and wrapped him in swaddling clothes, and laid him in a manger; because there was no room for them in the inn" [Luke 2:6-7, KJV].

(MARY *places baby Jesus in the manger while* JOSEPH *and the preschool choir look on. They sing an appropriate song. Part of the children's choir, dressed as* SHEPHERDS, *enter the platform area.*)

NARRATOR 3: "And, lo, the angel of the Lord came upon them, and the glory of the Lord shone round about them: and they were sore afraid. And the angel said unto them, . . ." [Luke 2:9-10, KJV].

LITTLE ONE: "Fear not: for, behold, I bring you good tidings of great joy, which shall be to all people. For unto you is born this day in the city of David a Saviour, which is Christ the Lord. And this shall be a sign unto you; Ye shall find the babe wrapped in swaddling clothes, lying in a manger" [Luke 2:10-12, KJV].

NARRATOR 3: "And suddenly there was with the angel a multitude of the heavenly host praising God, and saying, . . ." [Luke 2:13, KJV].

(CHOIR *sings appropriate song.*)

NARRATOR 4: "And it came to pass, as the angels were gone away from them into heaven, the shepherds said one to another, Let us now go even unto Bethlehem, and see this thing which is come to pass, which the Lord hath made known unto us. And they came with haste, and found Mary, and Joseph, and the babe lying in a manger" [Luke 2:15-16, KJV].

(SHEPHERDS *talk excitedly to one another. They move across the platform to the stable area. The* CHOIR *sings appropriate song.*)

NARRATOR 5: "Now when Jesus was born in Bethlehem of Judaea in the days of Herod the king, behold, there came wise men from the east to Jerusalem, saying, Where is he that is born King of the Jews? for we have seen his star in the east, and are come to worship him" [Matthew 2:1-2, KJV].

(WISE MEN *process down the aisle while* CHOIR *sings appropriate song.*)

Scene VII
All You Need Is a Willing Heart

(GABBY *and* LITTLE ONE *move to the center of the stage.*)

GABBY (*affectionately looking at* LITTLE ONE): Little One, I have never been more proud of you than tonight.

LITTLE ONE: Do you believe it, Gabby? All you need is a willing heart. How could something so simple be so hard for *me* to understand. I want everyone to know what I've learned. *(Pausing to think)* Maybe God will let me make special appearances all over earth so I can tell the Good News to everyone. Let's see, I could take the Brass Band and make stunning entrances before world leaders. Then . . .

GABBY (*laughing*): Little One, Little One. That's not God's plan. *(Points to the* SHEPHERDS) First the shepherds will tell their friends. Then at the Temple courts when Jesus is eight days old, Simeon and Anna will recognize that Jesus is the Messiah. Later . . .

LITTLE ONE: I know, I know. God's plan is for each person to tell someone else the good news about Jesus. It's a good plan. (LITTLE ONE *pauses when she sees* GABBY *with his [her] hands on his [her] hips looking very exasperated.*) No, it's the best plan.

GABBY: That's better.

LITTLE ONE: But do you think God would mind if I told the people *here* that God's plan is for them to tell the Good News?

GABBY: I don't think God would mind at all. Go ahead.

LITTLE ONE (*talking to the audience):* I've got a message for you. Each of you has a big job to do. And all you'll need is a willing heart. Will you join us in singing [an appropriate song]?

(Children process out during singing of final number.)

*CHORAL RHYTHMIC SPEAKING

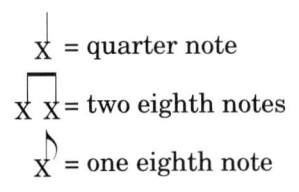

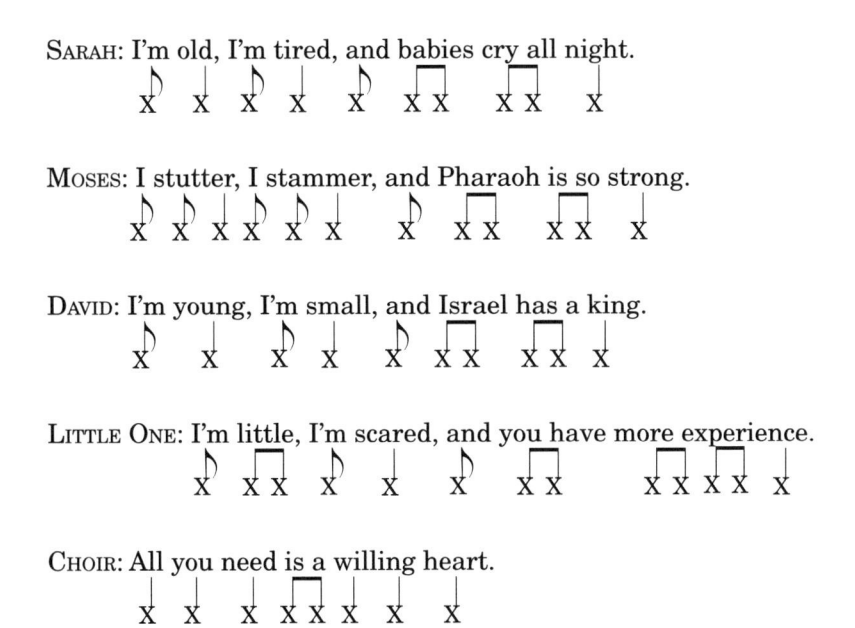

$\dot{x}$ = quarter note

$\overline{x\ x}$ = two eighth notes

$x^{\flat}$ = one eighth note

SARAH: I'm old, I'm tired, and babies cry all night.

MOSES: I stutter, I stammer, and Pharaoh is so strong.

DAVID: I'm young, I'm small, and Israel has a king.

LITTLE ONE: I'm little, I'm scared, and you have more experience.

CHOIR: All you need is a willing heart.